The Golden Age of Video Games

History, Impact, and Nostalgia

Table of Contents

Chapter 1. Introduction

Welcome to a thrilling journey through a time where creativity blossomed on digital landscapes and the line between reality and pixelated wonder started to blur! This Special Report, "The Golden Age of Video Games: History, Impact, and Nostalgia," invites you on an enchanting tour of the quintessential era of the gaming industry that changed how we engage with technology and each other. Prize-winning writers and industry veterans reunite to craft this masterful narrative, combining exciting historical analysis with delightful sprigs of nostalgia. Powered by riveting anecdotes, stunning visual galleries, and comprehensive data studies, this report is your portal back to the days when inserting a coin meant embarking on a galactic quest or saving a helpless princess. Even if you didn't grow up basking in the low-res, pixelated glow of the arcade machines, this report will make you feel a part of the ongoing, vast story of the grand evolution of video games. So, if you're hungry for nostalgia, yearning for how it all began, or merely curious about this digital revolution, this report is your must-have roadmap to the Golden Age of Video Games. Let the games begin!

Chapter 2. The Dawn of the Digital Era

Before we delve into the intricacies of the evolution and proliferation of video games, it is crucial to understand the environment that precipitated their inception. The late 1940s and early 1950s were a time of immense technological growth, marked by the advent of computer technology. This era spurred a profound transformation in multiple industries, from mathematics and physics to engineering and telecommunications, ultimately paving the path for the birth of the unconventional medium of entertainment called video games.

2.1. First Glimpses of Interactivity

The earliest known example of an interactive electronic game was developed in 1947 by Thomas T. Goldsmith Jr. and Estle Ray Mann. This game, patented as a "Cathode ray tube amusement device," was similar to World War II radar displays. It utilized an analog device to simulate a missile being fired at a target, the trajectory of which could be controlled by the user to "hit" different targets. However, due to the steep cost of the technology and its sheer size (approximately as massive as a piano), it didn't find its way into an average household.

Next in line to challenge the status quo was a physicist, William Higinbotham, who, in 1958, created "Tennis for Two," often credited as the first real video game. The game featured basic two-dimensional physics, allowing two players to volley a 'ball' across a simulated net on an oscilloscope screen. Though it wasn't designed with a commercial perspective, Higinbotham's creation stirred interest among his peers and public, proving video games' potential as an interactive entertainment tool.

2.2. Computing Machines: Uncharted Territory

However, the true birthplace of video games was a practical, albeit unexpected, one - universities. Research facilities and academic institutions were among the few places with access to the prohibitively expensive machines necessary for the development of video games. In 1962, a group of students at the Massachusetts Institute of Technology (MIT), led by Steve Russell, developed "Spacewar!"

This was the first game programmed for a digital computer rather than a dedicated console. Utilizing a machine called the Program Data Processor-1 (PDP-1), "Spacewar!" featured two player-controlled spaceships, the 'Needle' and the 'Wedge,' engaged in a dogfight while affected by the gravity of a central star. Despite the simplicity of its design, "Spacewar!" would go on to influence generations of games and gamers alike. Being publicly available for any MIT student, the game quickly gained popularity and was soon found on virtually every PDP-1 machine.

2.3. Advancements in Technology: Entering the Home

The cost and size of computing technology began to decrease due to advancements in transistor technology, bringing digital entertainment closer to the home. Magnavox, an American electronics company, capitalizing on this trend, released the first home video game console, the Magnavox Odyssey, in 1972. Designed by Ralph H. Baer, also known as "The Father of Video Games," the console could be connected to a standard television set and featured several gaming modes, including a digital version of table tennis.

Around the same time, Atari, founded by Nolan Bushnell and Ted

Dabney, introduced the world to "Pong," an accessible and engaging table tennis arcade game. "Pong" captured the attention and imagination of the public, resulting in a widespread smash hit.

2.4. A Fusion of Technology and Capitalism

The success of "Pong" marked the beginning of a new era of video games, triggering an avalanche of companies trying to capitalize on the new trend. Video games were no longer considered novel curiosities; they had morphed into lucrative entertainment products.

This transitional phase also saw the emergence of the first generation of game developers. Graduates from universities, armed with theoretical knowledge and a passion for gaming, began to form small teams to construct intriguing computer and arcade games. Among these youthful innovators were several who would go on to form monumental companies currently leading the gaming industry.

The fusion of technology and capitalism at the dawn of the digital era significantly influenced the trajectory of video games. The once academic clunky creations transformed into a polished mass-market product. It marked the point where video games managed to break free from the shell of obscurity and step into the limelight, kickstarting the golden age of video games.

As we move ahead, we will explore the games, people, and companies that built the foundations of an industry that would eventually become a cornerstone of global entertainment. Through their struggles and successes, we trace the steps of a relentless march towards technological innovation and cultural revolution, creating a unique spectacle, the echoes of which still resonate today.

Chapter 3. From Pong to Pac-Man: Rockstars of the Arcade

In the late 1970s, if one were to wander into any bustling arcade or family pizza parlor, enveloped in a cacophony of digital melodies and the excited chatter of competitive banter, they would inevitably spot two quintessential figures of the video game landscape: the immersive table tennis simulation 'Pong' and the pill-popping, ghost-dodging phenomenon that is 'Pac-Man'. These video game giants represented an entirely new form of entertainment, ushering an era teeming with pixels, polygons, and passion.

3.1. The Dawn of a Digital Classic: Pong

'Pong', released by Atari in 1972, wasn't so much a video game as it was a cultural earthquake. Born from the brain of Allan Alcorn under the guidance of gaming pioneers Nolan Bushnell and Ted Dabney, 'Pong' was simplicity incarnate. Two paddles, one ball bouncing back and forth, and the player with the most points at the end of the game reigned supreme. But even in its simplicity, or, perhaps, because of it, 'Pong' ignited a passion for video games across generations and cultures.

```
Players = "2"
Interface = "Dial"
Year = "1972"
Company = "Atari"
```

Its impact was immediate, installing 'Pong' in bowling alleys, bars, and video arcades across the globe. Suddenly, people who had never before interacted with a computer found themselves spending hours at 'Pong' machines, honing their skills until their names topped the high-score chart. More than that, 'Pong', with its competitive nature and accessibility, became a catalyst for community gatherings, instigating early manifestations of electronic sports.

3.2. Galactic Pursuits and Beyond: Innovations Post-Pong

With 'Pong' as the progenitor, a whirlwind of creativity found its way onto the gaming scene. Games like 'Space Invaders' (1978), 'Galaxian' (1979), and 'Asteroids' (1979) expanded on the simplicity that made 'Pong' such a hit while infusing the landscape with their own unique flavors.

The breakthrough of 'Space Invaders', with its relentless onslaught of alien invaders descending towards the player, put survival at the heart of gaming. 'Galaxian' took the concept further, adding diving enemies and multi-colored graphics. And 'Asteroids' gave players a different perspective, placing them in the middle of the screen with enemies coming from all sides.

```
Game = "Space Invaders"
Year = "1978"
Company = "Taito"

Game = "Galaxian"
Year = "1979"
Company = "Namco"

Game = "Asteroids"
Year = "1979"
Company = "Atari"
```

Gaming was suddenly a vibrant canvas teeming with creativity. In parallel, sound became an integral part of the gaming experience, whether it was the harsh blips and bloops of 'Space Invaders' or the thudding, ever-accelerating heartbeat that underscored 'Asteroids'.

3.3. A Colorful Revolution: The Birth of Pac-Man

The year 1980 bore witness to another seismic shift in the gaming industry, sculpted by Toru Iwatani, and named 'Pac-Man'. Its inception aimed to counter the somewhat violent nature of many arcade games, offering an entirely unique, non-combat experience. Arguably, 'Pac-Man' was the first video game with a protagonist, a character that players could guide through its neon mazes.

```
Player Character = "Pac-Man"
Enemies = "Ghosts (Blinky, Pinky, Inky, Clyde)"
Objective = "Eat all pac-dots while avoiding ghosts"
Power-up = "Power pellets turn tables on ghosts"
Year = "1980"
Company = "Namco"
```

'Pac-Man' was addictive, immersive, and highly social. The game's rock-paper-scissors mechanics, coupled with its vibrant aesthetics, ensured that it always drew a crowd. 'Pac-Man'also broadened gaming's audience, appealing not just to young boys but across age groups and genders.

This universal appeal catapulted 'Pac-Man' to mainstream fame, inspiring television shows, merchandise, and even a top ten hit on the Billboard Hot 100 chart. 'Pac-Man' wasn't merely a game – it was a pop culture phenomenon.

3.4. From Arcades to the Living Room: The Console Revolution

As the early '80s rolled around, the gaming titans towered over the arcade scene, their influence undeniable yet their reign not unassailable. The advent of home gaming consoles like the Atari 2600 and the Nintendo Entertainment System started fostering an environment where one could partake in their favorite digital pastimes without ever leaving the comfort of their homes.

Though initial attempts to translate arcade favorites on these platforms met with varying degrees of success, the development served as a harbinger of things to come. The dawning of the console age signaled a shift in concentration of power, from the buzzing arcades filled with change-ready machines to affordable consoles that could sit below your television.

3.5. Casting a Look Back: Legacy of the Arcade Era

Ultimately, the legacy of games like 'Pong' and 'Pac-Man' endures. Not because they were the first or the most popular, but because they're symbolic of an era that pushed boundaries and redefined entertainment, paving the road for what video games are today. This period of gaming history may have been short, but its influence stretches far, visible in every game, every console, and every developer that came afterward.

Looking back also reveals the seeds of current gaming trends. The social experience of arcades foretold the rise of multiplayer gaming and esports, while the simple, abstract graphics made way for the visually stunning landscapes of modern games. The obsession with high scores evolved into the progression and leveling systems that are commonplace now.

In essence, the era of 'Pong' to 'Pac-Man', the rockstars of the Arcade age, were foundational in constructing an industry that not only made a significant societal and economic impact, but also cultivated rich, unforgettable memories that still echo in the hearts of many. As the saying goes, to understand where we're going, we first have to understand where we've been, making this rosy journey down memory lane an enlightening exploration of our pixelated past.

Chapter 4. Joysticks to Keyboards: Transitioning to Home Consoles

The arrival of video gamings' golden age was accompanied by a significant transition: a movement from the commercially resonant joystick-based arcade games to the convenience and intimacy of home console gaming, where the ubiquitous keyboards became the new conduit of digital interaction. This move left an enduring impact on the industry, changing not only the economics, but also gaming practices and perceptions.

4.1. From Arcades to Living Rooms

In the early 1970s, video gaming was primarily a communal hobby played in arcades. These gaming hotspots known as 'Video Arcades' were filled with vibrant sounds of bleeps and blips accompanying the lively clang of coins disappearing into slot machines. The metallic joystick and vibrant buttons were the primary navigation and interaction tools.

However, this began to change in 1972, when Magnavox introduced the first home video game console named 'Odyssey'. Designed by Ralph Baer, known as 'The Father of Video Games', Odyssey had a simple design that required players to overlay screen graphics manually using plastic sheets on their television screens. It created a new pathway of gaming, making way for home-based consoles.

Historically, the journey from Joysticks to Keyboards was not immediately far-reaching. Throughout much of the late 1970s and early 80s, home consoles like Atari 2600, Intellivision, and Colecovision still utilized joystick-like controllers, merely transferring the arcade experience into the living room. Yet, this was a significant shift – from the public, vibrant, and social arena of the arcade, to the private, personalized environment of the home, providing gamers with a sense of ownership and control.

4.2. Bleeps to Syntax: An Interaction Transition

Once the setting changed, so did the manner of interaction. The joystick and buttons slowly gave way to the sprawling keys of a keyboard when home computers began to gain popularity. This change was marked by a paradigm shift in gameplay. From the rapid-fire responses required in arcade games, players now navigated text-based games, solving intricate puzzles or following deep narrative threads at their own pace, with commands typed directly into the game.

The leap to keyboard gaming was necessitated by the limitations of joystick controls with regard to their inability to match the complexity offered by various PC games. Games like 'Zork', 'King's Quest', and 'The Oregon Trail' required detailed input that a joystick couldn't provide. While the joystick was perfect for the shoot-'em-ups and chasing games found at the arcade, it fell short when it came to the text-heavy, strategy-involved PC games.

4.3. Commodore 64 and IBM PC

In 1982, when Commodore 64 was launched, it brought an affordable gaming-capable PC to a mass-market audience. It was packaged with a keyboard as the primary mechanism of interaction, thus sealing the keyboard's place in the home gaming set-up. Commodore 64 provided a simple BASIC language environment for programming, encouraging players to explore the world of game development.

In 1981, IBM entered the home computer market with the IBM PC, contributing to the transition from joystick to keyboard-focused gaming with its advanced hardware, which was compatible with a broad range of software. As more households welcomed home computers, the PC gaming environment burgeoned, offering complex narratives and interactive experiences, showcasing the keyboard's capability as a tool for nuanced gameplay.

4.4. Modern Controllers: A Hybrid Evolution

Throughout the 1990s and beyond, the controller evolved from a simple joystick to a complex interface device, effectively melding the binary enthusiasm of joystick buttons with the multifaceted expression of keyboard keys. Consoles like the Sony PlayStation, Sega Saturn, and Nintendo 64 showcased controllers with numerous buttons and multi-directional pads or analog sticks, offering an arcade-like finesse while retaining keyboard-inherited complexity.

This evolution continued into the 21st century with even more intuitive user interfaces, with controllers incorporating motion sensors (Nintendo Wii), touch-sensitive pads (PlayStation 4), and voice controls (Xbox One) making the gaming experience more immersive than before. These newer controllers also often offer keyboard-like functionality, embracing the versatility brought by this, now, classical input device.

4.5. Wrapping Up: The Legacy and the Future

From the joystick's arcade dominance to the keyboard's complexity, and finally to a hybrid controller allowing for a true experience balance, video gaming has seen a fascinating evolution in its interaction mechanisms. This transition has shaped the industry in immense ways, directly impacting the design of games, the nature of gameplay, and the economics of the industry.

The seismic shift from arcades to home consoles, and the subsequent change in the interaction paradigm, has created an enduring legacy that continues to define the industry. Looking towards the future, it's exciting to contemplate where technological advances might take these platforms. Regardless, this historical narrative - from flashing arcade lights to the warm living room glow, from metallic joysticks to tactile keyboards - will forever be foundational in the annals of the gaming industry.

Chapter 5. Nintendo's Revolution and the Rise of Mario

In the realm of video games, few names can match the widespread recognition and significance of the Japanese game company, Nintendo, and its mascot, an Italian plumber named Mario. To fully appreciate their impact, we must delve deep into the roots of Nintendo's history and the rise of this unlikely hero.

In the late 1970s, video games started to have a significant presence in homes worldwide with the introduction of home consoles such as the Magnavox Odyssey and the Atari 2600. While these systems did present a new level of accessibility and convenience, they were hampered by a lack of content diversity and low graphical fidelity.

5.1. A Gaming Giant is Born

It was within this context that Nintendo decided to enter the gaming industry. Having begun in 1889 as a playing card company, Nintendo had already survived several reinventions, and the late seventies presented them with another opportunity to transform. Seeing the potential that home gaming offered, the Japanese company started focusing on the development of its own game hardware.

Nintendo's first success came with the Game & Watch, a series of handheld LCD games introduced in 1980. Minoru Arakawa, the founder of Nintendo America and son-in-law to Nintendo president Hiroshi Yamauchi, believed there was a place for this new form of accessible, bite-sized entertainment. The small games, each with a unique simplistic algorithm, relied more on cunning design than graphical or processing power. They were instantly successful, creating a solid foundation for Nintendo to further explore the potentials of the gaming market.

5.2. From Arcade Success to Console Kings

In 1981, the company's trajectory skyrocketed with the creation of Donkey Kong, their first significant foray into the world of videogame arcades. They entrusted the game's development to a young artist named Shigeru Miyamoto. The young visionary was given a challenge - make a game that would sell in the wide and wild Western market.

Miyamoto broke away from the traditional space and war themes, creating a game narrative featuring a villainous ape absconding with a damsel and a hero rising to the occasion awash in a colorful construction site environment. This game introduced the world to the character who would eventually become an iconic mascot, 'Jumpman,' who later became known as Mario.

The success of Donkey Kong led Nintendo to further invest in home consoles, and in 1983, the company launched the Family Computer, also known as the Famicom, in Japan. The Famicom was revolutionary in numerous ways - musically engaging, with richer colours and sprites, and it opened the door to a more interactive, dynamic form of home entertainment.

5.3. The NES and the West

Nintendo saw both challenge and opportunity in the North American market, marred by the video game crash of 1983, caused by market saturation and loss of consumer trust due to low-quality games. In 1985, the company rebranded the Famicom, introducing it as the Nintendo Entertainment System (NES) in North America. Coupled with robust quality control and a strategic marketing campaign that positioned the console as a toy rather than a video game system, they were able to steadily gain momentum.

At the front of the NES's advertisement campaign was Super Mario Bros., developed by the same visionary behind Donkey Kong, Shigeru Miyamoto. Building on his success with Donkey Kong, Miyamoto created a vast, brightly colored world with intricate levels and detailed characters, igniting players' imaginations.

5.4. The Impact: Revolutionizing Gameplay

Super Mario Bros. went on to sell more than 40 million copies worldwide, making it the best-selling video game in history at the time and turned the plumber into a household name. The game revolutionized the platform genre, with fluid controls, recognizable character designs, distinctive level design, and memorable music. Mario's character design - a mustache to distinguish his nose, a hat to reduce the complexity of animating hair, and overalls to illustrate arm movements - was an intelligent move by Miyamoto, showing how limitations could be turned to advantages.

The Super Mario Bros. series continued to evolve and innovate, from the introduction of a nonlinear world map in Super Mario Bros. 3 to the groundbreaking 3D gameplay in Super Mario 64. Mario became a versatile character, starring in a variety of games from racing games like Mario Kart to RPGs like Super Mario RPG. As the mascot of Nintendo, Mario is now widely recognized and remains a significant figure in the industry.

Nintendo's legacy, built from the ground up by thoughtful design and a readiness to risk, has shaped the gaming industry's evolution and will not soon be forgotten. The rise of the NES, the boom of arcade gaming, the unparalleled success of Super Mario Bros., and the eventual establishment of home consoles as a dominant entertainment medium all manifest Nintendo's contributions in the gaming world. A guided nod to their vision, innovation, and an Italian plumber named Mario.

Chapter 6. Narratives and Role-play: Exploring New Dimensions

The convergence of narratives and role-play within video games marked a paradigm shift in the gaming world—usher-generating detailed universes populated by complex characters and intricate plotlines akin to substantial literary works. This advancement has resulted in a heightened level of engagement from players, inviting them to explore the personalities, backstories, and motivations of their virtual counterparts.

At its core, role-playing in video games propels the player into the heart of the narrative, effectively acting as the protagonist within the game's universe. By assuming a given role, one gains the power to influence events and, in many instances, dictate the trajectory of the story. Characters and quests stand as the bedrock of all RPGs (Role-Playing Games), offering emotionally charged experiences for players and paving the way for innovative storytelling techniques.

6.1. Mechanics, Structure, and the Evolution of RPG

From the 8-bit simplicity of the early titles to the sprawling, open-world masterpieces of today, RPGs have always been a cornerstone of the gaming industry. The first generation of RPG games was largely inspired by pen-and-paper board games like 'Dungeons & Dragons.' These classic games embraced the concepts of character growth, branching narratives, and player decision-making, translating them into digital form.

Although primitive by today's standards, they were monumental in defining essential aspects of the genre such as statistics, character class, and leveling systems. Games like Ultima and Wizardry set the stage for RPGs, establishing precedents in role-play mechanics and narrative structure.

These early RPGs imprinted on gamers the value of strategic growth—leveling up their characters, harnessing unique abilities, and crafting an arsenal of powerful artifacts. A sense of individuality began to permeate the genre. Each game's experience was unique, leading down to different paths, different narrative arcs. The player character was suddenly not just a virtual sprite, but a mirror of the gamer - every nobility, every flaw.

6.2. Effects of Choice on Narrative

The concept of player choice and its impact on the game's narrative has been an ever-present aspect in RPGs. In many of these games, players are faced with decisions that not only define their characters but drastically affect the game world itself.

Bioware's 'Mass Effect' series offers a myriad of narrative branches - all of which are completely dictated by the player's choice. The structure of its story was so intricate that choices made in the first game of the trilogy would hold repercussions in the final installment.

Even smaller titles like 'Undertale' pushed boundaries with multiple endings and gaming mechanics that purposefully subverted RPG conventions, delivering a strong, emotionally-driven narrative.

Choice in RPGs often puts ethics and morality into perspective. Games put players into difficult situations making them question their reasoning, their code. Are you the hero of your story or will you tread the path of an anti-hero? RPGs became a pool of introspective exercises, begging the question - What would you do if?

6.3. Narrative Depth and Character Development

Advancements in technology helped to significantly enhance narrative depth and character development in RPGs. The graphical capabilities of the later consoles and PC platforms enabled detailed character designs and impressive virtual world-building.

Developers began to concentrate on the formation of genuine personalities within the games. Through well-written dialogue and compelling backstory, NPCs (Non-Player Characters) transitioned from narratively flat sprites to characters with their own dreams, fears, and quirks.

Games like 'The Witcher,' 'Final Fantasy,' and 'Dragon Age' series are notable examples. These games exhibit storylines and characters with breathtaking emotional depth, often blurring the line between video games and traditional forms of storytelling like cinema and literature.

6.4. Legacy and Continuous Evolution

Decades after the birth of the first RPGs, the genre continues to evolve. Each title is a meticulously crafted narrative, a work of art, featuring personalized journeys that could last for hundreds of hours. With virtual reality and augmented reality creating immersive, tangible worlds, the genre is on the brink of another evolution.

To sum up, narratives and role-play in video games have managed to create a unique blend of storytelling and interactivity. They effectively bridge the gap between user and content, offering a deeper, more engaging experience. They've truly made the players the authors of their own unforgettable stories.

The future of RPGs is ripe with possibilities, promising adventures with new mechanics, deeper narratives, and characters that resonate with us more than ever before. For as long as the wheels of innovation keep turning, role-play and interactive storytelling will continue to shape the landscape of the gaming industry.

Chapter 7. Game Changers: Breakthroughs in Game Design

The evolution of video gaming is marred by numerous influential discoveries, ingenious innovations, and groundbreaking advancements - starting right from the 1970s right up to the end of the 1990s, the era fondly recognized as the "Golden Age". Venturing beneath the surface of this noteworthy period, our exploration starts with the critical breakthroughs in game design that fundamentally reshaped how we experienced games.

7.1. Picturing the Pixels

Video games, in the earliest days, were a stark contrast to the graphical marvels we see today. Understandably, the then existing low-resolution, single-color displays wouldn't impress anyone today. However, in the '70s, it was nothing short of revolutionary! These primitive video games were mostly created for academic or research purposes, lacking much appeal beyond their technical novelty.

The introduction of the pixel, a term coined in the early 1960s, had been brewing in the technological arena. Pixels, short for 'picture elements', were nothing more than tiny squares on the screen. The idea was simple: Combine vast amounts of pixels, each capable of displaying a different color, to create a broader picture. Imagine a digital mosaic, with every tile representing a pixel. However, the manipulation of these pixels to create compelling visuals was where the true artistry laid.

7.2. Dungeons and Dragons: Text to Graphics

While the use of text in games was both inevitable and innovative, the major leap from text-based to graphical interfaces was like stepping into another dimension. Although not entirely departing from text, games like 'Adventure' or 'Zork' offered a blend of both worlds. But, the memorable inception of the graphic adventure genre was initiated by the release of 'Mystery House' by Sierra Entertainment in 1980.

'Mystery House' was groundbreaking as it was the first adventure game to use vector graphics, transitioning away from a solely text-based interface. This, combined with intricate decision-making and multiple game endings, significantly changed the way games were both developed and perceived.

7.3. The Concept that Launched Millions: The Game Engine

The idea of a 'game engine' was primitive and nearly non-existent before the early '80s. Games were, frankly, hard-coded from scratch without any reusable code. This changed when Richard Garriott - also known as Lord British - developed the 'Ultima' series.

Garriott was the first to coin the term 'game engine.' The 'Ultima I' marked the beginning of this ingenious idea, which involved creating a set of reusable technologies for game development. This allowed developers to use the same underlying software to create different aspects of a game, drastically reducing the time required to code a game from scratch.

Simultaneously, another similar development was happening at Infocom, where the team developed a 'Z-machine,' letting game designers focus on the story and puzzles rather than technical details.

7.4. Seeing the World Sideways: Side-Scrolling Technology

If one were to pinpoint a video game design element that echoed through the ages, it would undeniably be 'side-scrolling'. While arcade games had previously been single-screen experiences, the introduction of side-scrolling technology presented a fundamental shift in game design.

'Space Panic' (1980) was technically the first game to introduce the side-scrolling concept, albeit in a simple form. But the true potential of this technology exploded onto the scene with the release of 'Jump Bug' (1981) and subsequently, the more well-known 'Super Mario Bros' (1985).

The innovative design of 'Super Mario Bros.' and its successful implementation of side-scrolling technology generated an endless, chessboard-like world teeming with challenges and adventures, spawning a virtually new perspective on game design.

7.5. Lifelike Immersion: The Advent of 3D

The 90s, while technically outside of what is often referred to as the Golden Age, heralded the advent of 3D gaming technology. Games started expressing depth, thus offering a more immersive experience filled with lifelike graphics.

Argonaut Software's Star Fox, released in 1993 for the Super Nintendo Entertainment System, made innovative use of the Super FX graphics acceleration coprocessor powered GSU-1. This pivotal development leveraged polygon-based rendering and introduced gamers to a new kind of visual experience.

Following this revolution, id Software's 'Quake' (1996) marked a milestone by featuring a fully 3D environment and characters, laying out the foundations for the first-person shooting (FPS) games we universally love today.

Video game design was indeed a flux field in the Golden Age. It was a period of rapid and revolutionary changes, with each breakthrough paving the way for the next. The untamed creativity and relentless pursuit for innovation of the pioneers mentioned here, coupled with countless others, shaped the principles and practices that have grown into the familiar norms of our beloved gaming world today.

Chapter 8. The Impact of the Golden Age on Pop Culture

The broad brushstrokes of the golden age of video games painted an entirely new reality, opening spaces previously unimagined and flinging wide the doors of creativity and expression. These years, typically marked as the mid-1970s through 1985, were the eras when video games shifted from niche, technophile hobby to a force in pop culture that surged like a tsunami. Their impact was deep, wide-ranging, and has been reverberating till date.

8.1. Changing Definitions of Entertainment

Before the advent of the golden age of video games, entertainment was largely passive. Audiences watched films, read books, or listened to music. They were receivers, not creators or participants in these mechanisms of diversion. Video games changed that by offering a means of interaction, a way for the consumer to influence the narrative outcome directly.

Pong became a landmark game when released in 1972 by Atari Inc., helping to establish the video game industry. It offered an entirely new manner of consuming entertainment, pitting players against each other in this early simulation of the classic game of table tennis. For the first time, screens were not there to be merely gazed at, they were there to be engaged with.

Games such as Spacewar!, and later Space Invaders (Taito Corporation, 1978), thrust the players into throbbing cores, brimming with danger and challenge. These experiences shook the public's understanding of what a pastime could entail and provided a fresh perspective on engaging with a narrative.

8.2. Impact on Art and Aesthetics

Video games played a part in molding factors beyond the realm of amusement and idle time. They influenced art and aesthetics, creating an entirely new avenue for artistic expression that did not rely on conventional forms. Pixels became the brush strokes, and the black canvas of the video screen became the medium.

The ascent of pixel art, epitomized by icons like Pac-Man (Namco, 1980), rescripted cultural symbols of the era. This new artistic direction was later adopted by numerous subcultures in arts and aesthetics.

More so, video game soundtracks added a new flavor to the music scene. The mesmerizing melodies of games like Super Mario Bros. (Nintendo, 1985) and The Legend of Zelda (Nintendo, 1986), despite their technological limitations, became fan favorites and were often recorded and shared, reinforcing the widespread popularity of this new art form.

8.3. Social Paradigm Shift

Prior to the rise of console gaming and arcades, digital entertainment was limited to a select few—the 'geeks' who understood computers enough to fiddle with them. The democratization of games altered the societal view of digital entertainment. Arcades became gathering spots, no longer exclusively inhabited by the technologically savvy. The simple charm of games like Ms. Pac-Man (Midway Games, 1981) reached across gender lines, painting a more inclusive picture of gaming.

The competitive social dynamics of video games fostered new bonds between people, tying them together in the struggle to reach higher levels or attain high scores. This dynamic created a shared experience, a common vernacular of power-ups, extra lives, and boss fights that permeated everyday conversation.

8.4. Merchandising and Economical Impact

With the rapid proliferation of video games, companies saw opportunities to monetize this new cultural wave. Consumers flocked to stores not only for games but also for merchandise associated with their favorite titles. Toys, apparel, lunch boxes, and even breakfast cereals carried the likenesses of popular characters.

Moreover, games truly flaunted their economic muscles during this era. Just between 1978 and 1979, arcade coin-op machines revenues in America lept from $1 billion to a staggering $2.8 billion, giving Hollywood and the music industry a run for their money.

The eruption of the arcade culture and home consoles during this era had profound macroeconomic implications, leading towards a vibrant and revolving industry responsible for thousands of jobs and immense economic activity globally.

8.5. The Lingering Influence

Measured by the potency of its echoes, the golden age of video games altered the course of pop culture like few other events have. It touched and altered entertainment, art, social interactions, and commerce. It handed the joystick to the engaged consumer, making them an active participant in the narrative, and in the process, redefined what entertainment could be.

Today, video games have evolved into an industry that harpoons through the clutters of the digital age. They're the bridge between generations old and young, fostering common ground in a shifting, uncertain world. Their powerful influence, initially unfurled during their golden age, continues unabated, constantly reshaping the contours of pop culture.

Chapter 9. Gaming: A Social Phenomenon

In the nascent days of video gaming, the act was predominantly solitary in nature. You against the machine. The man, so to speak, against the digital beast. A dystopian aspect yet with a sense of excitement and raw challenge. It was far off the current social extravaganza we have come to associate with the term gaming. The transformation didn't happen overnight nor was it unexpected. It was the evolution fueled by a blend of technology, society's needs, human creativity, and a dash of serendipity.

9.1. The Early Seeds of Social Gaming

The earliest arcade machines represented a battle between humans and AI, metaphorically represented by elusive pixels on the screen. Even though these single-player games were the core draw, social engagement sprouted around them. They were housed in arcades, where the atmosphere was more dynamic and community-oriented, fostering the first sense of social gaming. Game enthusiasts would swarm around a popular machine, taking turns, competing for high scores and establishing an unspoken camaraderie.

Fast forward to the late 70s, the introduction of multiplayer games embedded within a single game console started setting a solid bridge between gaming and social interaction. Games like Pong and later Combat on the Atari 2600, offered a two-player mode that allowed friends, siblings, or parents to compete from their living room. Gaming finally had transcended a one-on-one duel between man and machine to include human opponent(s). The living room warfare was the start of gaming becoming a shared activity, multiple hearts throbbing with thrill simultaneously over a common digital quest.

9.2. Exploring Friendships and Discovery via Split-Screen Co-op

In the 80s and 90s, split-screen co-op gaming took center stage. Titles like Contra on the NES, Golden Axe on the Sega Genesis, and the iconic Mario Kart series on various Nintendo systems, allowed two or more players to share a screen and either work together or compete against each other. This era was riddled with team collaborations, fierce friendly-rivalries and in-person socialization. A noteworthy mention is the impact of games like The Legend of Zelda: A Link to the Past had on gamers, inspiring them to share tips, secrets, and gameplay strategies with their peers, though they were essentially single-player.

9.3. Multiplayer Gaming and the Birth of MMOs

The Internet became a game-changer, quite literally, for the social aspect of video gaming. As dial-up connections slowly started making way into homes, the concept of Massively Multiplayer Online games (MMOs) started emerging. Ultima Online and Everquest were some of the early starters, creating a dazzling virtual universe where players could be part of quests, raids, and social alliances, all in real-time across the globe. The most significant contribution of MMOs was the establishment of robust gaming communities that transcended geographical boundaries. The blend of narrative, role-play and societal structures within the games provided players with an enriching social experience. This new-age digital space led to friendships, rivalries, and alliances often stronger than ones in reality.

9.4. Current Role of Social Bonds in Gaming

Social bonds in gaming continued to evolve and spread across a wide array of game types. Multiplayer Online Battle Arenas (MOBAs) such as League of Legends and Dota 2 have built complex communities that include not just players but fans who spectate, discuss strategies, and follow their favorite players closely. In recent years, games like Fortnite, PUBG, and Among Us have taken social gaming to another level, with interactive gameplay, cooperative structures, and global, real-time battles. Today, the social experience has become a critical aspect of video games, reflected not just in multiplayer gameplay but also in the discussion forums, Reddit threads, live Twitch streams, and e-sports tournaments.

9.5. Impact on Societal Norms and Culture

The role of video games as a social phenomenon has far-reaching implications, shaping societal norms, culture, and our perception of reality. Through MMOs and virtual reality, cultures mix, social norms evolve, and biases get challenged. Virtual economies, social structures, and governance in games such as EVE Online have mirrored, and in some cases influenced, their real-world counterparts. Studies have also shown the potential of video games as tools for social learning, improving empathy and advocating for social causes. Gamification, a product of the gaming revolution, is now a crucial tool in education, business, and wellness programs, reinforcing how the gaming industry's seeds have grown into a mighty tree of societal influence.

This is the palette of the social landscape of gaming – extraordinarily colorful, inspiring, and engaging. Tracking this journey of how video games transitioned from solitary engagements to being meticulously entwined with our social fiber paints a promising image of the future. Games are no longer about the escapism they once offered. It's about intertwining our lives with the digital world, leading to the possibility of immersing oneself into an alternate reality, yet never disconnected from our human roots.

Games are no longer just games, but social platforms - communities that foster friendship, collaboration, competition, and cultural exchange. This exploration isn't simply about understanding the past, but also about foreseeing an exciting journey for mankind, merging with technology in ways one could only dream of during the inception of these pixelated wonders. Welcome to the social phenomenon of gaming. Enjoy the ride.

Chapter 10. Pixels to Reality: The Evolution of Game Graphics

In the early days, video game graphics were unadorned, monochromatic sequences of blocks. The digital characters that occupied the television screens were mere figments of light, far from any semblance of reality. Fast forward to today and you might find yourself trying to distinguish a real cityscape from a computer-generated one, such is the detail and precision of modern digital representation. The trek from mere pixels to startlingly true-to-life replicas with breathtaking graphics forms the heart of this discussion.

10.1. Birth - The Demise of Text and Rise of Pixels

Before the advent of bona fide graphics, text games dominated the digital landscape. Titles like Zork and The Oregon Trail mesmerized players with their walls of text and command-based inputs. The game graphics' first evolution, however, saw this text-dominated narrative paradigm shift dramatically.

With the launch of Pong in 1972, the game changed. It introduced the world to graphical video games with an interface that, although primitive by today's standards, was revolutionary for its time. Pong was endearing in its simplicity: a dot bouncing back and forth, two paddles, and numbers to track the score. The rudimentary pixel-based graphics became a staple of early video games, paving the way for future advancements.

10.2. Sprites - The Dawn of a New Era

From Pong's simple dot and paddles, the gaming industry leaped forward with the invention of the sprite: a two-dimensional bitmap that could be manipulated as a standalone object in the larger graphic scene. In 1978, Space Invaders swept the gaming world, employing sprites to depict both invaders and player spaceships.

Indeed, the sprite technology reached its zenith with the release of the influential *Super Mario Bros.* (1985) by Nintendo. This game, with its vividly colorful worlds, well-defined characters, and engaging gameplay, is still widely regarded as a masterpiece of sprite-based graphics.

10.3. The Jump to 3D - Polygons and Beyond

Sprites ruled the 80s, but polygonal graphics were the next quantum leap. Early experiments in 3D games like Battlezone (1980) introduced gamers to wireframe graphics, which gave birth to primitive 3D visuals. However, it was the introduction of the *Star Fox* game on the Super Nintendo Entertainment System that propelled polygonal graphics to the front row.

I, Robot (1983) also holds a special place in history as it is arguably one of the earliest commercial games to use filled polygons. But the real revolution in using filled polygons for characters and environments came with breakthrough titles like *Virtua Fighter* (1993), which showcased characters with individual body parts, and *Myst* (1993), which astounded players with its photo-realistic rendered environments.

10.4. The Console Revolution

The 1990s also saw the birth of the PlayStation, which brought 3D games to the domestic market. Gamers were thrilled with the likes of *Final Fantasy VII*, *Metal Gear Solid*, and *Resident Evil*, which offered immersive worlds made possible by sophisticated polygon-based 3D graphics.

Around the same era, the Nintendo 64, with titles such as *Super Mario 64* and *Legend of Zelda: Ocarina of Time*, authored a defining chapter in console-based 3D gaming, offering an unparalleled interactive experience with their mesmerizing graphics, sprawling worlds, and intricate gameplay.

10.5. The Advent of GPUs

The advent of the Graphics Processing Unit (GPU) was a significant milestone in gaming history. Before GPUs, CPUs had to bear the brunt of rendering. NVIDIA's invention of the GPU in 1999 with the GeForce 256 was a landmark moment. The GPU offloaded the rendering work from the CPU, introducing hardware transformation and lighting and freeing up CPU resources. GPUs bolstered the rise of advanced shading and lighting techniques, thereby dramatically improving gaming graphics.

10.6. High Definition and Photorealism

Modern gaming has entered an era of high-definition graphics and photorealism that was once thing of the wild imagination. Titles such as *The Witcher 3: Wild Hunt*, *Last of Us Part II*, and *Red Dead Redemption 2* offer beautifully rendered, life-like environments teeming with detail—so much so that they might even deceive a casual observer into mistaking the on-screen for reality.

The rise of physical-based rendering (PBR), which leverages complex shading algorithms to replicate how light interacts with different materials, has pushed realistic game graphics even closer to the cutting edge.

10.7. Future Prospects: Virtual Reality and Beyond

As we gaze into the future of video game graphics, virtual reality holds enormous potential. With immersive technology becoming increasingly pervasive, the division between real and digital will blur further.

While real-time ray tracing—an advanced lighting technique that simulates how light works in the real world—has been the talk of the town, it's only the beginning. Incremental advancements in GPU technology, AI-assisted rendering, and high-resolution displays will continue to push the boundaries of what's possible in video game graphics.

In essence, the evolution of game graphics from elementary pixel-based designs in the 70s to the photorealistic environments captured in the latest titles has been a remarkable journey. As technology continues to advance at a blistering pace, we can only anticipate what breathtaking innovations lay on the horizon for video game graphics.

Chapter 11. A Glance Backward: The Nostalgic Allure of Retro Games

The siren call of chiptune music, the high-octane thrill of an 8-bit car chase, the agonizing defeat by an unassuming pixelated plumber — for many of us, these are the memories that never cease to delight, fascinate, and captivate, no matter the years that stretch between then and now. The allure of retro games isn't purely a matter of nostalgia, but a throwback to a simpler time when game design was in its infancy, and when creativity and innovation in gameplay mechanics, narrative elements, and visual style often overrode high-resolution graphics or complex AI systems. Let us take a journey back to this pivotal time in gaming history and analyze the enduring appeal and influence of these pixel-based pioneers.

11.1. Exploring the Pixelated Past

At their core, retro games exemplify a dimension of video gaming that often gets forgotten in today's graphically rich, 3D-rendered environments - gaming isn't always about realism, but about the experiences offered through the medium. Games like "Space Invaders," "Pong," or "Pac-Man" delivered simple yet addictive gameplay mechanics that kept players hooked for hours. The developers oriented themselves around the core of what makes games enjoyable: an invigorating challenge, clear progression, and, most importantly, fun. Their simplistic design has enabled these games to persist in our collective memory, setting the foundation for further innovation in the gaming industry.

Retro games developers also had to work with highly constrained hardware and resources. This pushed them towards ingenuity and sheer creativity that is now hardly a necessity because of the availability of technology. The pixel art aesthetic we recognize and love today originated from these hardware limitations, as developers aimed to portray as much information as they could within a limited amount of screen space. The 8-bit color schemes and 16-bit sprites are testaments to the creativity fostered by constraints; the games from this era remind us of how less can truly be more.

11.2. The Nostalgic Appeal of Familiar Characters

Much of the nostalgia surrounding retro games can be attributed to the recognizable characters and franchises that we have grown to love. The triumphant rise of the plumbers Mario and Luigi, Link's heroism in the land of Hyrule, and the fiery battles of "Street Fighter" were instrumental in creating these strong emotional bonds. The continued appearances of these characters in contemporary games, the fan fictions, the series, merchandise, and adaptations keep these flame of memory alive, perpetuating our connection to the golden days of gaming.

Video game characters, like characters in any other form of media, have a significant role in the player's personal development. Many of us remember drawing strength from characters like Samus or Mega Man, deriving inspiration from their courage in facing insurmountable obstacles. These characters become a part of our personal narrative, symbols of resilience and determination that we carry with us into adulthood.

11.3. The Evolution of Retro Gameplay

The gameplay of retro games, despite the simplicity, is quintessentially what draws people back to them time and again.

These games focused on offering players a means of escape and adventure without the requirement of a high learning curve. You could pick up a controller and start playing immediately, whether it's the straightforward action of Pac-Man munching on dots or the more complex mechanics of The Legend of Zelda's puzzle-solving.

Modern games possess a complexity that some might find distancing. With convoluted controls and intricately layered mechanics, the current generation of games can be intimidating for the uninitiated. Retro games present a counterpoint to this trend, providing straightforward gameplay that's easy to learn but hard to master. They offer a level of accessibility that enables anyone, regardless of skill level, to engage in the game world.

11.4. Legacy and Renewed Interest

While the current generation of video games offers unforgettable experiences, the relentless march of technology often leaves us pining for the games of our youth. The retro gaming community has, over the last decade, witnessed a resurgence, appealing to both old-time fans and newcomers alike. Remastered versions of classic games, retro gaming consoles, and even mobile adaptations of old titles have tapped into this renewed interest and nostalgia for the classics.

Retro gaming isn't merely a quaint artifact from the past; it's a potent, persistent subculture that provides the blueprint for many current gaming trends. The ongoing indie gaming boom, with its penchant for pixel art and chiptunes, draws heavily on the aesthetics and mechanics of retro games. Furthermore, many viral successes, such as Flappy Bird, have reaffirmed the enduring appeal of simple yet challenging gameplay.

Whether you're an old timer reminiscing about the lost afternoons spent at the arcade, or a kid dazzled by the simple brilliance of pixel art, retro games hold a unique allure. From the strain of overcoming a high score to the thrill of pixelated duels, these experiences and characters form the foundation of our collective gaming story. Indeed, the allure of retro games lies in this; our shared history, etched into cartridges and arcade boards, and its profound impact that shaped our digital landscape. It's a testament to how far we've come, and the wonders we are yet to discover.

www.ingramcontent.com/pod-product-compliance
Lightning Source LLC
Chambersburg PA
CBHW071038260726
48661CB00007B/3045